PRAISE FOR
BEING WHOLE (Inside Your Own Skin)

Everyday life is full of stress that can be difficult to manage. Our emotions complicate our responses. This book provides effective bite size ways to respond to those feelings, leading to a happier and more productive life. Your copy awaits for immediate benefits.
—*Maria R. Urbano, MD*

Find self-acceptance here on the complex journey of living, in small well-crafted steps. Brilliant, beautiful, and yours to use in whatever ways suit you: pick it up, set it down, mull it over. The reward of curious, courageous self-exploration is being more comfortable in your own skin and more skilled with others. I'm grateful for this resource to use personally and professionally.
—*Lisa Tedeschi, MA, LMFT*

So timely! Simple steps to build resilience during difficult times.
—*Kathleen O'Connor, M.A.*

BEING WHOLE

(Inside Your Own Skin)

BEING WHOLE

(Inside Your Own Skin)

Radiance, Balance, Resilience, and Depth

Suzanne Gregg, PhD

Anamcara Press LLC

Published in 2025 by Anamcara Press LLC
Author © 2025 Suzanne Gregg, PhD
Book Cover Art by Jeff McLure
Photography by Bruce Bischoff
Book design by Maureen Carroll
Eras Demi ITC, Minion Pro, Minion Pro, Lithos Pro.

Book Description: In just one quiet minute a day, discover greater emotional clarity, resilience, and peace. Dr. Gregg's gentle, insightful reflections guide you through life's complexities with compassion and wisdom.

ANAMCARA PRESS LLC
P.O. Box 442072, Lawrence, KS 66044
https://anamcara-press.com/

Ordering Information:
Quantity sales. Special discounts are available on quantity purchases by corporations, associations, and others. For details, contact the publisher at the address above.
Orders by U.S. trade bookstores and wholesalers. Please contact Ingram Distribution.

Gregg, Suzanne, Author
Being Whole, Inside Your Own Skin:
Radiance, Balance, Resilience, & Depth

PSY013000   PSYCHOLOGY / Emotions
OCC019000 BODY, MIND & SPIRIT /
Inspiration & Personal Growth
SEL042000   SELF-HELP / Emotions
SEL021000   SELF-HELP / Motivational & Inspirational
SEL024000   SELF-HELP / Self-Management /
Stress Management
ISBN-13: 978-1-960462-64-0 (Paperback)
Library of Congress Control Number: 2025942506

To Drew, Kim, Stan, Carole, and Ron.
To my granddaughters: Emma, Elizabeth, and Alison.
To my goddaughters: Meagan, Melanie, and Sreydy.
To Dante, whose life is a dedication to resilience.
To all we've lost too soon, in loving legacy.

Contents

Foreword

Emotional challenges are complex, especially in our times, but they do not have to be!

Being able to provide advice to parents about childhood behavior was one of the most challenging aspects of practicing as a children's doctor for nearly four decades. However, having the calm, reassuring voice of Dr. Gregg to provide my most challenging cases with the advice needed was always a Godsend.

Over the years, I came to appreciate her ability to distill life's complexity into steps even the most harried parent could take. Parents were dealing with their own emotions while attempting to corral the emotions of their child, with the child's health and emotional resilience at risk. Future well-being and happiness were at stake, which only her years of study and practice could help guide appropriately.

Even if you've never raised children, the developmental threads here are the same for you. You can become more at peace with your thoughts and feelings by taking advantage of Dr. Gregg's wisdom distilled from her years in practice. Allow yourself the relatively small investment of time needed to sort your emotions daily. With her experience and your newfound resilience to guide you, the depth of your own wisdom begins to reduce life's complex challenges. You gain deeper purpose in your daily emotional connections with yourself and others.

—*C. Steve Vinson, M.D. (Retired)*

Author's Welcome

Welcome, to the curious! I'm glad you are holding this book. Along with you, I'm trying to make sense of it all, this being human in a complex world. Sometimes it all seems too much to bear, inside my own skin. This led me to a deeper search, one I'm happy to share with you.

My field is developmental psychology. It is the study of human development from birth to death, from cradle to grave. Each person is alive in their own unique way over a lifetime, facing opportunities or obligations at every step, and changing course when necessary.

I've enjoyed reading and writing day and night since second grade, when my military family returned to the U.S. from an assignment in Japan. The class was already reading and writing in cursive, so I found myself behind, struggling. I grew to fill a diary as a child, wrote letters to cousins as a teen, entered poetry contests in high school. I moved on to blue book essays in college, journals galore, a dissertation in grad school, national presentations as university faculty, and international presentations as medical school faculty.

With an unquenchable interest in human nature, I've been gathering material from good literature as well as academic sources. Biographies were among my favorite reading selections, along with stories of heroism, redemption, and second chances. And, like you, many lessons came from my own life experiences, from joyous family celebrations as well as dark nights of disappointment and distress. I've learned that good authors are as insightful as good psychologists in examining and understanding human nature.

We gather wisdom along the way, some from our successes and some from our failures. Some come from master teachers and some from quiet introspection. Most of all, I've learned that Life is the consummate Master Teacher. It doesn't help to rail against reality. What was, was. And what is, is. Our only option is, what's next? For that we move to hope, inspiration, and creativity. The discovery awaits!

Introduction

"To know thyself is the beginning of wisdom."
—Socrates, philosopher

No one lives a perfectly balanced life. Yes, we have strengths, though maybe not on all fronts. Yes, we have triggers or calamities we must address. There is always something that trips us up, especially in the places where we are most vulnerable. The goal is to be okay, *inside your own skin.*

Along with you, I am a student of this human experience, still learning the breadth and depth of it. Like you, I am no stranger to pain, upheaval, and confusion. Like you, I know what it's like to feel sorrow, to suffer, to doubt, and to rant. Life ebbs and flows, like a revolving door of joys and sorrows. It is tempting to pull away and shut down when life gets tough. Hopefully we recover, aided by natural delights, simple pleasures, and exuberant joys. We only wish that it could be faster, easier.

What you will find here is a simple way to discover that you are far more than you ever dreamed. With *one quiet minute* of self-study, you can discover another layer of who you are. Each minute you invest in yourself pays you back with a richer, deeper understanding of yourself and your place in the world.

Once you realize the full extent of who you are, it opens you to a new level of understanding. There is no need to banish any of your feelings or mood states. You might, however, come to regulate them better. We are all a work in progress, flaws and all. Knowing the full breadth of your emotional makeup is the first step towards living with greater ease.

Being human, you are alive with thoughts and feelings. Some thoughts are helpful, some are not. You can rein in some unceasing thoughts. Some feelings are nurturing, some are not. Feeling every feeling is your birthright. You can also learn to tame some feelings before they erupt into inexcusable actions.

Each day, you can begin to step through a minefield of thoughts and feelings and remain intact. Or you can fail to do so and suffer instead. From a busy life in a chaotic world, one way to find calm and gain balance is to quiet the noise. When you practice simple ways to manage repetitive thoughts and overwhelming emotions, you preserve your sanity and ensure your wellbeing.

With *one quiet minute* of *self-study*, you can shift into a life of less stress, less reactivity, and more ease. This is a book of *brief reflections*. It offers you a way to sort through the clutter, to claim all that is essentially yours, and to right-size the rest. You can hold every emotion as your own, for example, yet loosen the grip of self-doubt, self-judgment, fear, and blame.

This is not a book about being perfect. It is a book about *being whole*. The task here is simple, but not easy. Make peace with your own journey, with its joys, its obstacles, limitations, and setbacks. Build strength and resilience. I can help you define the territory. Using these tools, you will continue to unearth the roadmap to a life that is uniquely yours. Yours is a life worth living with clarity and ease. Starting now.

On Being Whole

"Always remember that you are absolutely unique.
Just like everybody else."
—Margaret Mead, anthropologist

It comes as no surprise that you most likely understand yourself in fragments. You can see yourself as a child, a teen, a sibling, a student, a friend or lover, a parent, a boss, your work role, or your artistic side. Perhaps you've been a braggart, a helper, a donor, a guide, or someone trusted, adored, attacked, or despised. Your focus is often consumed by one of those roles at a time. It is far more difficult to keep in mind that perhaps you've been all of this, on different occasions.

Whatever you've come to believe as yourself, you are in fact so much more. Finding the whole of you includes your disagreeable tendencies as well as your sterling qualities. You can't be blind-sided when you accept that you display, at times, every known belief, emotion, or mood state. It's an honorable search. The whole of you is far more intriguing than any of your sole separate identities.

Being whole means being human…flaws, radiance, and all. Being whole requires a wider embrace of self and world and circumstances than usual. An impromptu self-review might generate an either/or descriptor. Either you are strong or you are not, smart or not, shy or not, scared or not. In truth, being whole is more likely a result of being both/and. Both approachable and not, sometimes. Both kind and not, sometimes. Claiming this, you begin to live large, as all that you truly are.

Being whole gives you a particular kind of freedom. Even as you take steps to widen your perspective, it is hardest to resolve conflicts on the edges and in the depths where you feel most vulnerable. Over time, you will gain the most ground in places where you fear you have the most to lose. I can shrug off any number of insults and put-downs, as not personal enough for me to lose sleep. Yet if I am blamed, for example, over my mistakes, I am undone. Who wouldn't want to be coached rather than blamed? Once I allow that I'll be blamed, sometimes, and I cannot silence the critic, I'm no longer hostage to their dagger. There is freedom in this. You can gain that same level of freedom, inside your own skin.

Just be who you are suited to be. Others can be who they are suited to be. The world needs one of everybody. They need what you bring as much as you need what they give. Your exact mix of interests, talents, and personality is vital to meeting the needs of all. The whole world benefits when you live your own version of what is right and good and just and true for you.

Inside This Book

"Knowing others is intelligence; knowing yourself is true wisdom." —Lao Tzu, philosopher

Think of the way that light and shadow create an image. Light without shadow is a blank sheet. Shadow without light is a black slate. The interplay between light and shadow makes you whole, even interesting. This self-study is a discovery of what steadies you and what makes you tremble. You learn that troubling emotions first signal threat or danger to help keep you alive. You learn, too, that uplifting emotions can act as comfort against the sting of troubling emotions. Learning the language of emotions, intricacies and all, helps you secure your place in a world full of complexity. It's a topic rarely taught in families or schools.

You are aiming to allow the experience of each belief, emotion or mood state named in the reflections. There is no need to purge any of your emotions. They belong to you. Your goal is to see them for what they are and let them inform you. They are meant to serve you, not to rule you. You need enough information to make peace with your own emotions but not too much that it hijacks your ability to think and plan and act. You hold the reins to your life in your own hands.

Use the language here to speak to your deeper self. The phrasing, set out for you in the reflections, is designed to interrupt intrusive mind chatter by inserting pauses. This is not the scroll of daily news, nor the familiarity of dialogue, but something far more personal. It is the voice of psyche that reverberates through you and alerts you to something known on some level but never fully faced. Psyche is a still, small, interior voice that holds the truth of your entirety instead of merely your splintered sides of self.

In *Minding the Body, Mending the Mind*, Joan Borysenko said that her "ideas represent the synthesis of a collective wisdom that is as old as humanity itself." That synthesis is also available for you here, in compact form. Use it to settle yourself from the inside out, no matter the outside circumstances. In one quiet minute at a time.

How to Use This Book

Read. Think. Feel. Learn. Practice. Heal.

This book has two parts, *Landscape of Emotions* and *Living the Wisdom*. With the chapters in Part One, Radiance and Balance, you survey and study your strengths and your struggles over beliefs and emotions that impact you daily. The chapters in Part Two, Resilience and Depth, aid you in discovering the ways wisdom arises in your own life. There are *brief reflections* in each chapter designed to support you in your *self-study* of all that you are.

In Chapter 1, the *Radiance of Uplifting Emotions*, you learn to amplify the personal values that set the foundation of your life, lived on your terms. You can survey nurturing emotions, offered here in alphabetical order. In Chapter 2, you explore how to rightfully *Balance Troubling Emotions*. You learn to address the pitfalls and stumbling blocks that threaten to upend your daily experiences. Your survey of distressing emotions is offered here in alphabetical order for easy guidance.

It takes rehearsal and steady practice to develop a new habit, either healthy or unhealthy. Befriending all sides of yourself is the healthy version, resulting in sanity and well-being. Feel the satisfaction of uncovering another layer in your foundation as you study each reflection.

You might read each reflection in Part One to set the tone for your day. Rest assured that there is no wrong way to use the material presented here. Dabble, if you wish. Pinpoint specific emotions, if needed. Or read through each reflection with the structure given. Finding your own best routine will aid you in making this a steady practice, since steady practice leads to mastery.

The alphabetical format of reflections in Chapters 1 and 2 gives you easy access to specific emotions, if needed for further self-study. For example, if you face a daunting obstacle, turn to Tense in Chapter 2, or turn to Ease in Chapter 1 to choose a path that offsets tension.

Once you more readily grasp your underlying beliefs, emotions, and mood states from Part One, start observing your shift to wisdom in day-to-day life with the reflections in Part Two. Chapter 3 helps you build *Resilience* in the face of real-life challenges. In Chapter 4 you probe the *Depth* of insight necessary to contain it all. You might use the reflections in Part Two to settle you before sleep. Your last thoughts of the day help set the tone for your mindset upon awakening.

Give yourself the *Gift of Time,* in bitesize pieces, to discover what the *whole of you* entails. Find *One Quiet Minute* to invest in your ultimate wellbeing. If you have the luxury of a quiet minute over morning coffee, great. Or you might need to *steal* a minute from the headlong rush of a day, perhaps while sitting in the car before driving off. You might need to *trade* a minute, from mindless scrolling or channel surfing, to devote to yourself.

Obligations and distractions abound. Commitment waxes and wanes. Every minute, however acquired, that you invest in fully knowing yourself pays immediate dividends. You begin to uncover the wisdom to live your life on your own terms with far more grace and ease. That is priceless.

To Begin

Read the selected reflection and listen as it echoes through you. Find what resonates, what is welcome and familiar, or what triggers your vulnerabilities. Let the message settle and guide you. Carry the thought with you and notice when examples arise. Doing this strengthens your recognition of that specific experience.

Each repetition of the reflection takes you through deeper layers of your psyche, shifting you from thoughtless reactivity to reflection and understanding. You can hear the same message in a variety of nuanced ways over time. One hidden benefit of nuance is how the one version that specifically matches your need is like turning a key in a lock. You are far more open to that one message, the one that speaks to your inner needs.

You can use the journal lines, if you wish, to record your examples and to watch your level of mastery shift over time. Use alternate methods like a sketchbook, voice recording, or video format, if you prefer. Your goal is to discover how to shift from being a Reactor in your life, inflamed by every provocation, to being a Witness, able to pause and select your personal best response. There is no absolute perfection in you, in others, or in your world as you know it. With a wider perspective, you can live as yourself just as you are, with others just as they are, in an unpredictable world just as it is.

PART ONE:

Landscape Of Emotions

"You have been told that, even like a chain, you are as weak as your weakest link. This is but half the truth. You are also as strong as your strongest link."
—*Kahlil Gibran, poet*

Introduction to Part One

Your self-study of the human condition begins with a startling fact. There are hundreds of emotions, perhaps 400 or more, well known to poets and philosophers. This should come as no surprise to us, but it does! It helps explain how you can easily be blind-sided by emotions you can barely name. Notice how often in a day you and I are swamped, side-tracked, and triggered by strong emotions pressing us to pay attention. It also relieves you of a burden, thinking that you should be better at getting a grip on your life. It is hard to keep your balance when you are bombarded from all sides, more sides than you ever guessed.

Two possible reactions to this barrage would be unhelpful to you. One is to block all sense of your feeling states and walk through your days on autopilot. The other is to escalate every emotion into a drama, impacting you and those around you. These choices end up causing you physical and emotional distress and even disease over time. You could instead choose a method that helps ensure your well-being in a chaotic world.

Gaining practice in learning to navigate the territory of beliefs, moods, reactions, emotions, and feeling states is a response more helpful to you. Study the path of early brain development. Infants display five core emotions from an early age: joy, sadness, fear, disgust, and anger. Long before we have the capacity for language and reasoning, we have emotions. Long before we can name them and understand them, we have strong emotions. Even from birth, we are wired to register more distressing emotions than comforting ones, on a scale of four to one.

You can see how the deck was stacked from the start! Year by year, you link additional nuanced emotions to each of the core five. Sadness, for example, shifts into loss and loneliness and emptiness and longing, among others.

When it is chronic, it can downshift into a state of depression. Each of the core five unfold, like a fan, into the full array of human emotions. From 5 to 400 or more emotions! You are left to cope as best you can.

When you take time to survey the full landscape of emotions, you have a better chance to be okay, *inside your own skin*. Use this self-study to learn how to quiet the noise from self-criticism, self-blame, and expectations. Judgment can be a major stumbling block. Judgment of others using outrage and insult, or of yourself using shame and blame, disrupts your peace and well-being. Imperfections are a sign of your shared humanity. Embrace them, along with your strivings.

The reflections are quick-reads, easily inserted into a demanding life. Brief reflections help you steadily learn about yourself and your world. You begin to understand what keeps you afloat and how to safeguard those lifelines. You learn to adjust your viewpoint after gaining a wider perspective. And you learn when you need more time for deeper reflection because the issue at hand is multi-faceted or seems insurmountable, like unresolved grief or unexpected failure. Begin now.

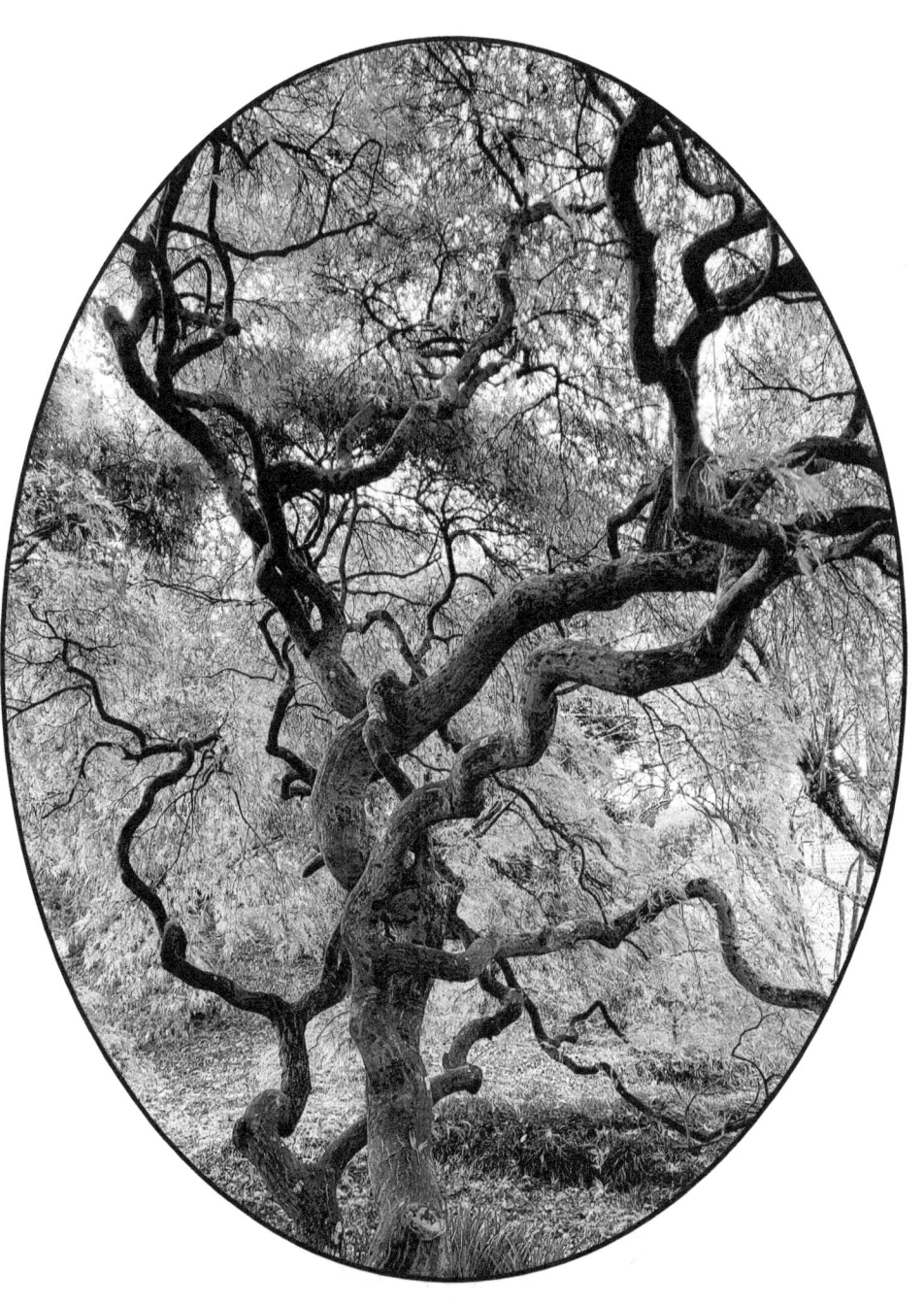

Chapter 1

 ## Radiance of Uplifting Emotions

Every atom in your body came from a star that exploded. It really is the most poetic thing I know about physics: You are all stardust."
—Lawrence Krauss, theoretical physicist and cosmologist

Your brain is designed to scan for danger, to keep you alive. This leads you to focus first on what is wrong with yourself and your world. Draw instead on the heart strengths here to calm this alarm, feel soothed, and find balance, over time. There is a glow about you, a sparkle, a radiance noticed by others when you choose to focus on the best in yourself and others and your world. This takes practice. Steady Practice helps you develop a ready alternative to being stressed, enabling you to connect to deeper resources which help protect you against feeling overwhelmed.

Every moment of uplift helps counteract the downward pull of fear and anxiety. Steeped in practices like joy, gratitude, empathy, and compassion, you can shift your focus beyond the continuous loop of distress and despair. Reorienting throughout the day leaves you less time to be flooded by intrusions like fear, anger, anxiety, and shame. As you practice, others will notice. They might unknowingly repay you in-kind, reflecting your goodwill back to you. Win/win.

Start the day with a purpose. *Slowly breathe in a sense of expansiveness, aware that you are far more than you believe moment to moment.* Read the selected reflection and listen as it echoes through you. Find every opportunity to express the uplifting emotion named in the reflection. Watch and listen for that feeling state to be displayed by others, when you meet them in person, on social media, or in print. Notice the times you naturally express that emotion as you go through your day. Then watch for further opportunities to embody that emotion, times you might have missed without the focus of this exercise. End the day by recording something notable from your self-study, in a new sense of ease, perhaps, or in particular feedback from others. Remember, you express as your own every radiant emotion.

Radiate ACCEPTANCE Today

Of life on Life's terms. Of progress and setbacks, of order and chaos. See reality come to your door, knowing you can adjust when needed.

_____

_____

_____

_____

_____

Embody ALTRUISM Today

There is great need in every corner of the globe. Equal to yours. Extending selfless goodwill to others enriches you as well as them.

_____

_____

_____

_____

_____

Embody BALANCE Today

A foot in each camp. Work-rest, job-family, mine-yours,
fast-slow, go-stop. Always be mindful of the midpoint.
Return to center when needed.

_____

_____

_____

_____

_____

Embody BELIEF Today

In innate goodness, both yours and theirs. In possibilities,
still unknown at this moment. In right outcomes, meted
out to all, in the end.

_____

_____

_____

_____

_____

Radiate CALM Today

You can't stop a storm with insults and rage. Find comfort
and ease instead. At the eye of the storm there is a calm
center. Live there.

_____

_____

_____

_____

_____

Radiate CARING Today

You see your neighbors burdened by their cares, which can multiply. Sharing and caring lightens their load and revives their spirits.

_____

_____

_____

_____

_____

Embody CLARITY Today

Life is messy, complex. Hold firm in your clear motives, words, and vision. Others benefit along with you, watching you sort out the tangles.

_____

_____

_____

_____

_____

Embody COMFORT Today

Words that soothe, beliefs that uplift, a glance that reassures. Take comfort in a slower pace, in the simplicity of what you seek and what you offer.

_____

_____

_____

_____

_____

Embody CONFIDENCE Today

The answers you seek are often deep within. Turn there.
Trust that you have the necessary skills. The rest will
come to you as needed.

_____

_____

_____

_____

_____

Radiate CONNECTION Today

Make eye contact; extend a smile. Call each person you
know by name. Find the warmth of familiarity with each
one you meet.

_____

_____

_____

_____

Embody CONSOLATION Today

There are many earthly reasons to lament. No need to put
on a false front. Console yourself first with self-soothing.
Then console others.

_____

_____

_____

_____

_____

Embody CONVICTION Today

Stand firm in your own values. Express your beliefs without shaming others. Believe that good will prevail, given time and opportunity.

_____

_____

_____

_____

_____

Embody COURTESY Today

Extend courtesy often because everyone struggles, often in secret. Surprise others, being willing to assist, without keeping score.

_____

_____

_____

_____

_____

Radiate CURIOSITY Today

Be curious about old paths and ancient ways. Stay curious about new discoveries. You exist, keenly alive, no matter your age or ability.

_____

_____

_____

_____

_____

Embody DARING Today

Dare to dream, dare to create. Dare to speak up, to speak out. Dare to risk, to fail, to try again. New worlds await. Dare to reveal your true nature to someone.

_____

_____

_____

_____

_____

Radiate EASE Today

There are two paths to every goal, both effort and ease. Ease in, ease back. Find your pace, smooth and steady. Effortless, at ease.

_____

_____

_____

_____

_____

Embody ECSTASY Today

Delight in the tender touch, the heart-stopping exchange. Breath-taking beauty is all around. Just stop and look, to be transported, rapturous!

_____

_____

_____

_____

_____

Embody ENERGY Today

Spring arrives, all comes alive again. Life and hope and rebirth abounding. Live life energized, replenished, filled to the brim, as if from Earth itself.

_____

_____

_____

_____

_____

Radiate ENTHUSIASM Today

For everyday tasks, that support daily life. For challenges, that open something new. For teamwork, that is affirming. There is much to gain.

_____

_____

_____

_____

_____

Embody FAIRNESS Today

Wanting for everyone what you want for yourself. Shielding everyone from what you'd shield yourself. Everyone gains, feeling equal.

_____

_____

_____

_____

_____

Embody FAITH Today

That you are in the right place. That humanity rises to the greater good, that good will prevail. With faith that all will be well one day.

_____

_____

_____

_____

_____

Embody FIDELITY Today

Be true to yourself, your dreams, your vision. Be true to your word, both your Yes and your No, that you give to others. They are reassured.

_____

_____

_____

_____

_____

Embody FORGIVENESS Today

To yourself, once young and often imprudent. To others, as no one masters everything. Everybody blunders, but they are far more than that fiasco.

_____

_____

_____

_____

_____

Embody FORTITUDE Today

Stay the course, even on rough patches. Life's zigzag path at times requires grit and pluck. Dig deep. Hold firm to your steady resolve.

_____

_____

_____

_____

_____

Radiate FORTUNATE Today

Sufficient food for your meals. Your work is appreciated. The traffic flowed, without incident. Count all that worked out in your favor. At least for today.

_____

_____

_____

_____

_____

Embody GENEROSITY Today

Give more than money, give freely, and often. See the needs, yours and theirs. Give of your time, your love, your support, your encouragement.

_____

_____

_____

_____

_____

Radiate GENTLENESS Today

There is strength in being gentle. Moving with, not against, the ideas and choices of others. Unopposed. Holding theirs and yours in equal measure.

_____

_____

_____

_____

_____

Embody GRATITUDE Today

For beauty, in people and in places. For kindness and tenderness. For setbacks, that teach crucial lessons. Each helps to offset life's sting.

_____

_____

_____

_____

_____

Radiate HAPPINESS Today

Moments of happiness are stepping stones in the murky river of life. No need to pursue them. Show delight when they appear! Pure pleasure.

_____

_____

_____

_____

_____

Embody HARDINESS Today

Be stalwart, sturdy, robust, even in adversity, equal to the challenge. Shift to mastery or seek advisors; change direction, if needed, for growth.

_____

_____

_____

_____

_____

Radiate HARMONY Today

Find the place in you that warms to each person. To some portion of each idea, each incident. You might need to stretch; you'll benefit.

_____

_____

_____

_____

_____

Embody HEALING Today

For all your broken places, your dis-eased body parts. For the rifts in all your relationships. For our towns and cities, our fragile planet. All are in need.

_____

_____

_____

_____

_____

Embody HONESTY Today

Speak your truths, in big ways and small. Revise them as
new facts arise. Sometimes silence is the best truth. Or
speak up for those with no voice.

_____

_____

_____

_____

_____

Radiate HUMOR Today

Be more than your serious side. People are quirky; laugh
with them. Life is messy. Let mirth bubble up, as depths
of hilarity get sparked.

_____

_____

_____

_____

_____

Embody INSPIRATION Today

Inspire others, as you were once inspired. To be kind, to
do good, to show compassion. To create the best for all in
a world of possibility.

_____

_____

_____

_____

_____

Radiate JOY Today

Over the smallest treasures, of travel to the greatest vistas, or delightfully astonishing surprises. To the steady heartbeat of Being Alive one more day.

Embody JUSTICE Today

In a just world, all are safe, all find shelter. All are heard; listen to both sides, support each as needed. All have worth; give respect.

Embody KINDNESS Today

Share an easy smile, a kind word, a kind deed. Especially powerful when unasked, unexpected. Like balm for a live-wired nervous system.

Radiate LAUGHTER Today

Laugh like a four-year-old at the jokes of a nine-year-old.
Find what's funny in the human condition. That scatters
the clouds blocking the sun.

_____

_____

_____

_____

_____

Embody LONGING Today

For deeper understanding. For wider perspectives and
possibilities. To create a future of full participation, meeting the needs of all.

_____

_____

_____

_____

_____

Radiate LOVE Today

Not just to the lovable, as that is easy. It's the unlovable
who need it most. Open up to all; share your heart. Love
is the only answer.

_____

_____

_____

_____

_____

Embody MERCY Today

To the undeserving, give the benefit of the doubt. For a fresh start. For yourself when you feel undeserving. Extending to all without fail.

_____
_____
_____
_____
_____

Embody NURTURING Today

Someone you know needs a human touch. Or a hot meal, or food for thought, or sustenance through difficulties. Maybe you do?

_____
_____
_____
_____
_____

Radiate OPENNESS Today

Embrace new ideas, new discoveries, new territory. Open to change. This expansive new you exists beyond the routine and familiar.

_____
_____
_____
_____
_____

Embody PATIENCE Today

In traffic, on the phone, in long lines. Picture the serenity of a sheltered cove for yourself; wait there. Wish it for the impatient, too.

_____

_____

_____

_____

_____

Radiate PEACE Today

Create a peaceable kingdom, in your mind and heart, with family and friends. In conflict? Try forbearance first, staying centered.

_____

_____

_____

_____

_____

Embody PERSPECTIVE Today

An unchanging point of view can get stagnant, out-of-date. Like a prism, shift to see events from another angle. Open your mind to it.

_____

_____

_____

_____

_____

Radiate PROTECTION Today

Protect your mind and heart, your faith and vision, your family and your neighbors. Protect the unprotected; all will benefit.

_____
_____
_____
_____
_____

Embody QUIETING Today

Steal a moment of stillness from a busy day. Luxuriate in it. Slow down, narrow your gaze; listen for your own heartbeat, your own inner thoughts.

_____
_____
_____
_____
_____

Radiate RESPECT Today

For those lowly or those mighty, those outcast, down-trodden, those indigent, or impaired. Show honor to each person, regardless of their circumstances.

_____
_____
_____
_____
_____

Embody SANCTUARY Today

Offer a safe harbor, calm and soothing, to all who seek respite. Let no harm cross your threshold; stand guard against direct and indirect threats.

_____

_____

_____

_____

_____

Embody SOOTHING Today

Life can be a rocky road. Counter with gestures meant to settle rather than perturb yourself and others. A self-hug is as necessary as air and water.

_____

_____

_____

_____

_____

Radiate SPACIOUSNESS Today

Under stress, vision narrows, responses constrict. Look around, scan horizons. Tap into all the vast resources there; feel enlarged.

_____

_____

_____

_____

_____

Embody TENDERNESS Today

People wither under harsh treatment. Bypass censure, soften to your tender core. Treasure yourself and others, with deep care and compassion.

Embody TOLERANCE Today

Just as we try to truly fathom those we love, we can also try with those unlike us. Tolerate tensions and misunderstanding, as if seeing no stranger.

Radiate TRUST Today

That something good happens somewhere in the world every minute. That new solutions will be found. This can expand, multiply, and magnify.

Embody UNDERSTANDING Today

That each person lives first from their own upbringing, and second from further learning. That words may hold different meaning. Take time to listen.

Radiate UPLIFT Today

Surf the rising tide of possibility, lifting all. Turn the wheels of progress, in your own domain. Speak encouraging words, yours as well as theirs.

Embody VISION Today

Envision the best for yourself and all humanity. You can refuse to settle, as others have before you. We all gain a better world, a better future.

Radiate WARMTH Today

Gather those you love and treasure. Surround them with your caring embrace, with the intensity of your love. Then extend this further.

_____

_____

_____

_____

_____

Embody YES Today

Yes, I'm here. Yes, I will listen, comfort, support. Yes, you can count on me. You can even inconvenience me; I won't refuse or strike back.

_____

_____

_____

_____

_____

Radiate ZEST Today

Life is meant to be lived fully. Nature is ripe with beauty, earth a cornucopia of bounty. Live this one life with zest, good for body and soul!

_____

_____

_____

_____

_____

Chapter 2

✠ Balance Troubling Emotions

"This being human is a guest house.
Every morning a new arrival.
A joy, a depression, a meanness,
Some momentary awareness comes
As an unexpected visitor,
Welcome and entertain them all.
Treat each guest honorably.
He may be clearing you out
For some new delight." —Rumi, poet

Our ancestral DNA was constructed in response to a harsh world of danger and threat, with risks to survival at every turn. All emotions are messengers. It's common for us to refer to positive and negative emotions. When we assign a judgment to distressing emotions, though, we further fuel our tendency to recoil, avoid, and repress them. Over time, we gain no advantage from keeping on our blinders.

Troubling emotions, maybe 300 or more of the 400 named emotions, play a crucial role in alerting you to physical and emotional threats. You can easily be confounded by strong emotions. Of the multitude at play in your daily life, it serves you well to examine those that afflict you. When you begin to decode and untangle them, you discover that they coexist in multiple, deeper layers. Anger, for example, might be a secondary emotion to the primary insult of humiliation. Feeling adrift might be a companion emotion to the triggering emotion of grief following loss.

Your goal is to harvest the messages these emotions carry, not to banish or to bury them. For some you need only notice and name the emotion, register its existence, and move on. For others you may need to delve further, evaluate the level of threat, then find resources to address them. Each time you bristle or clench, use that as a signal to avert or buffer the surge of unbridled reactivity ahead. With study, you gain perspective, right-size those out-of-scale emotions and find a better balance.

To be okay deep inside, taking stock on your sunny days is of little benefit. To be okay in stormy times as well as serene is the true measure of being whole. There is freedom in this, even though the territory is vast. The most interesting people you know are complex, multi-faceted, and at times contradictory. You are learning to be the most interesting person you know.

Start the day with a purpose. *Slowly breathe in a sense of expansiveness, aware that you are far more than you believe moment to moment.* Read the selected reflection and listen as it echoes through you. Find every opportunity to notice the troubling belief, emotion, feeling, or mood state named in the selected reflection or recall a time when it unsettled you. If any emotion feels too raw to address, set it aside for later. It's better to build a strong foundation with supportive emotions first.

Watch and listen for the expression of that experience by others, whether in person, on social media, or in print. Notice the times you naturally express that emotion yourself as you go through your day. Practice right-sizing the impact of that disturbance in your life, using the reflections here to do so.

End the day by recording something notable from your self-study. Perhaps you moderated your own reactions or de-escalated ongoing conflicts with others. You are enlarged rather than diminished by every possible emotion, whether pleasant or unpleasant. This is *being whole.*

Observe, Consider, Relive, or Recall as you Reflect on each of the following.

Note Being ABANDONED

Left out, left behind. People move away, move on, cut off. Many chambers in the heart sit empty. You can revisit each in memories, those never lost.

Note Times of ADVERSITY

Fire, flood, storm, injury, attack. Not under your control. Bemoan the plight, but conserve energy for coping. No story about it, just one step onward.

Recall Feeling ANGRY

A signal that someone, something is an obstacle, working against you. You power up to counter it! Try downshifting to evaluate, then problem-solve.

Recall Feeling ANXIETY

Life has many demands. We tense up with fear, worry, doubt. Can we measure up, keep up, deliver? Let it all unfold. "They" can't eat you.

_____

_____

_____

_____

_____

Recall Often BEMOANING

The hard knocks, the harsh fallout. Downcast, comparisons up, never down, the ladder of success. Ride it out, by viewing the whole picture.

_____

_____

_____

_____

_____

Recall Feeling BETRAYED

By those enjoined to protect, entrusted with your deepest secrets, or whose affections waned. Offset this with personal integrity, regardless.

_____

_____

_____

_____

_____

Recall Feeling BEWILDERED

Arrays of choices, opinions, and options multiply daily. Which to choose? Follow the narrow path that is more yours than someone else's.

_____

_____

_____

_____

_____

Recall Feeling BLAMED

For something you did, or something you didn't. For not knowing, for forgetting. Maybe the blamer was blamed. Accept responsibility, not blame.

_____

_____

_____

_____

_____

Note CAUSTIC Remarks

A biting remark, cut-throat actions; meant to scorch, incinerate. Leave it alone; do not reply in kind. Disinterest eases its sting, do not engage.

_____

_____

_____

_____

_____

Recall Feeling COMPLACENT

Rooted in status quo, tunnel vision, limited to the familiar. Turn instead to help just one neighbor, to show caring. Your world begins to expand around you.

_____

_____

_____

_____

_____

Recall Feeling CONFLICTED

You want to and you don't; to act or not act. Delay, for clarity. If pressed, consider the cost/benefit of each option. Be willing to pay the price.

_____

_____

_____

_____

_____

Recall Feeling CONFUSED

A flux of ideas, beliefs, opinions, no road map. Who can say? Watch those you respect, whose lives you emulate. Revise and adjust, upwards.

_____

_____

_____

_____

_____

Note Times of CRAVING

Something you desire, can't get it out of your mind, can't
ignore its magnetic pull. Try the one-minute delay, then
extend to two. Take pride in setting it aside.

_____

_____

_____

_____

_____

Recall Feeling CRITICIZED

On how you look, act, walk, talk, think, and deliver. Who
appointed the critic? Revel in being who you are, flaws
notwithstanding. You matter, just as you are.

_____

_____

_____

_____

_____

Recall Feeling DESPAIR

There is no likely solution in sight. Bleak on all fronts.
Watch as the prism shifts; you see more clearly the realm,
the range, of possibilities.

_____

_____

_____

_____

_____

Recall Feeling DEPRESSED

Overcome by sorrows? No delight in simple pleasures? Shift first to the beauty of earth and the majesty of heavens. Side by side, hope follows.

_____

_____

_____

_____

_____

Recall Feeling DISCOURAGED

All your efforts go sour, all trial-and-error fails. No approval, no openings. Set it down, walk around, give it time. The remedy is not yet known.

_____

_____

_____

_____

_____

Note Times of DISGRACE

Learn from mistakes, sure. But some are so egregious that you are avoided, shunned. What now? Need distance to rebuild, newly aware.

_____

_____

_____

_____

_____

Recall Feeling DREAD

That lurking sense of doomsday, of the firing squad. Yet millions have felt that way and lived. Study their lives. At the end of the tunnel, picture a door.

Note Times of DRUDGERY

New day, same tasks; this comforts some, not you. Routine, tedious, tiring. Look around. Always something new out your window to uplift, inspire.

Recall Feeling ENVY

You see what they have, you want what they have. Look further. Perhaps they lack something you value more? Reassess.

Note Times of FAILURE

No one is born knowing everything; we learn by trial-and-error. Failing stings when compounded by derision from others. Begin again, undaunted.

_____

_____

_____

_____

_____

Recall Feeling FEARFUL

Something dark and foreboding, coming for you. Worst-case scenario looms. Shift from freezing up and cowering to just one possible next step.

_____

_____

_____

_____

_____

Recall Feeling FOOLISH

Another misstep, even when you know better. Buying into a fantasy, entranced by the cheap, the fake. See it as whimsy, not reality.

_____

_____

_____

_____

_____

Recall Feeling FRENETIC

Life at warp speed, overwhelmed. Increasing demands
for more, faster, sacrificing better. For a minute, lay your
burdens down, take a cosmic view.

_____

_____

_____

_____

_____

Note Times of FRICTION

Push and pull, it's all abrasive. No one budges, nothing
settles. Step off the seesaw sooner rather than later. No
need to play the game; find your ease.

_____

_____

_____

_____

_____

Recall Feeling FRIGHT

Onslaught, attack, assault, outnumbered; no avenue of escape available. Safeguard the spark of life-force to survive.
In time, your wounds can heal.

_____

_____

_____

_____

_____

Note Times of FUTILITY

Every effort blocked, no solutions work. Shift to flow like water. Find a different goal, a different task to tackle. Return to this one later, renewed.

_____

_____

_____

_____

_____

Recall Feeling GREEDY

Grasping, stockpiling, always wanting more. There is never enough to fill your emptiness. In reality, less soothes. Carry only as much as you need.

_____

_____

_____

_____

_____

Recall Feeling GRIEF

Ache, anguish, heartache. Loss, tragedy, collective trauma. All will never be the same again. Being broken can open deep wells of caring.

_____

_____

_____

_____

_____

Recall Feeling GUILTY

Over all transgressions, great and small. Face responsibility, take action. Make amends when you can, before it festers into a toxic mix.

_____

_____

_____

_____

_____

Note Times of HARM

Attacks, not just piercing the skin, but also the heart. Spare the knife, the thoughtless barb. Protect every one of us, from even one hurtful thing.

_____

_____

_____

_____

_____

Recall Feeling HATEFUL

Overblown reactions to someone, something not-like-me. Pull back, reconsider. Make room for reflection, clear mind and clear heart.

_____

_____

_____

_____

_____

Recall Feeling HAUNTED

Shadowed by images that don't fade; gripped by dark memories. Crushed by words on a continuous replay loop. That "then" is not "now." Blink.

_____

_____

_____

_____

_____

Recall Feeling HELPLESS

No resources to cope, no way to succeed, no vision. Only when we stand together do we have it all. Link arms, accept help, give and receive.

_____

_____

_____

_____

_____

Recall Feeling HUMILIATED

Your transgressions made public into the light of day. Sullied, cannot erase the dirt. Use this anguish as stairsteps to your growth, your wholeness.

_____

_____

_____

_____

_____

Note Being HUNGRY

For food, for love, for attention, for favor. What will nourish you? Deeper reservoirs quench more needs. Giving opens more room for receiving.

_____
_____
_____
_____
_____

Recall Feeling HYPOCRITICAL

What you say versus what you do, does not align. As if rules only apply to others, not to you. Sharpen your personal lens, revise this, often.

_____
_____
_____
_____
_____

Recall Feeling IGNORANT

Knowledge is not static, never absolute. Modify false facts, erroneous beliefs. Revise the spreadsheet daily; tally wisdom, new discoveries.

_____
_____
_____
_____
_____

Recall Feeling IGNORED

Not seen, not heard, even when in the same room. This causes exquisite pain. Step onto a different stage. Be fully yourself, your own true self.

_____

_____

_____

_____

_____

Note Often IMPATIENT

Come now, move now, serve me, answer me. But good ideas, deep thought, right actions take time, to bring satisfaction. Tolerate waiting.

_____

_____

_____

_____

_____

Note Times of IMPUNITY

It's tough to watch those who disregard edicts. To trust that sanctions will be applied, fearing they won't. Your one reminder: do not elect to imitate.

_____

_____

_____

_____

_____

Note Being INCONVENIENCED

Plans go awry. Pressing needs override your vision, goals.
Fuming only adds a second stressor. Making it personal
aggravates you; set that aside.

_____

_____

_____

_____

_____

Note Times of INFERIORITY

Less than, not enough, can't measure up. Who says?
Change voice, or scorecard, even domain. Be "just right"
as yourself; no need to be another.

_____

_____

_____

_____

_____

Recall Feeling INSECURE

No safety net, no sense of belonging, no way forward. Re-
boot. You belong to yourself, just as you are. Claim your
own place in your life, not theirs.

_____

_____

_____

_____

_____

Recall Feeling INSENSITIVE

Hasty words or actions protect you but wound others.
Hard to always gauge. Add one step: listen to yourself.
Rethink; keep the dialogue open.

_____

_____

_____

_____

_____

Recall Feeling IRRITATED

It's all too loud, too crass, too dismissive. Tasting the
poison of that, you can shift out of it. Neutralize its power
over you; set up a shield.

_____

_____

_____

_____

_____

Recall Feeling JADED

Cynical, indifferent. Seen it all, can't be bothered with the
mundane. Revive curiosity, into the unknown. Explore a
new direction, a new territory.

_____

_____

_____

_____

_____

Note Times of JEALOUSY

Each person is unique, true to themselves. Why be jealous? Proud of them, proud of yourself, doubles your joy, your excitement, and your elation.

_____

_____

_____

_____

_____

Note Times of KILLJOY

Demeaning joy sours one's disposition, deflates one's hopes and dreams. With nothing to gain, much is lost. Find uplift, delight, child-like, not childish.

_____

_____

_____

_____

_____

Note Times of LAMENT

Forces stacked against you, scenes of inhumanity around you. First you weep, then notice, roses still bloom. Both/and, these always coexist.

_____

_____

_____

_____

_____

Note Times of LIES

Those you hear, those you tell, the ones you tell yourself. Each steals integrity, true essence. Put on the brakes now. Unearth truths daily.

_____

_____

_____

_____

_____

Recall Feeling LIMITED

By place or station, energy or opportunity. Living one single life script? Be limitless in tender mercies. In love, joy, peace, patience. For self, for others.

_____

_____

_____

_____

_____

Recall Feeling LONELY

Even in a crowd. For long-gone places and people, for compatibility. Reach out, befriend someone or something new to you. This creates a Win/Win.

_____

_____

_____

_____

_____

Note Times of LOSS

Dreams fade, relationships fizzle. Pets die, people, too.
All are established facts. Grief is inevitable. In time, seed
fertile ground for new growth.

_____
_____
_____
_____
_____

Recall Feeling LOST

Unmoored, can't get your bearings. Even the familiar
looks strange; no fit for you there. Perhaps this is a time
just to wander, find new trails.

_____
_____
_____
_____
_____

Recall Feeling MANIC

Too much, too fast, never done, never enough. Rushed,
wanting more, until depleted. Settle now, tune in, dial
back, to nourish and to restore.

_____
_____
_____
_____
_____

Recall Feeling MEAN

Mean-spirited, mean thoughts, mean words. Yours? Or passed on to you from others. Try again, kindly. This can even open closed doors.

_____

_____

_____

_____

_____

Note Being MINDLESS

Sleep-walking through your day, on autopilot. Following the crowd, absence of goals or values, copying theirs. Start small, notice. Just. This. Moment.

_____

_____

_____

_____

_____

Note Being MISTAKEN

Vehement opinions, way off track. Judgments fully formed but flawed. A touch of humility leaves a window open for truth, and rights the wrongs.

_____

_____

_____

_____

_____

Recall Feeling MOODY

Hot and cold, you or others. All over the map, pulled in every direction. Of many minds, muddied. Gather all the reins, then proceed, enlarged.

_____

_____

_____

_____

_____

Recall Feeling NUMB

Avoidance is common. We detach to escape, to go unnoticed, To not feel the grip of reality. Practice saying: "This Hurts, but I am undiminished."

_____

_____

_____

_____

_____

Note Being OBSESSED

With someone or something, with status or acclaim. Mind on a fixed loop. Limit the grip of fixating, reapportion the day, add in a mix of delights.

_____

_____

_____

_____

_____

Recall Feeling OPPRESSED

Subdued by others, by their edicts. Using harsh moral strictures to bind, no give. Untie the knot. Ideas and people both need breathing room.

_____

_____

_____

_____

_____

Note Times of OUTRAGE

Over hearing insults hurled. Or seeing injustice and inhumanity. Helpless in the face of broken systems? Investigate, join others seeking change.

_____

_____

_____

_____

_____

Recall Feeling PAIN

Physical pain, mental anguish, heartbreak. Bemoaning your plight doubles your pain. Streamline, hold only the original ache. Until it passes.

_____

_____

_____

_____

_____

Recall Feeling PESSIMISTIC

The world's a mess, broken, backwards. The future looks bleak. Note how often opportunities arose from unlikely sources throughout history.

_____

_____

_____

_____

_____

Recall Feeling PETRIFIED

Wolf at the door, physical threat. Legal woes, emotional blackmail. Link to strong supports while you sort it all out. To buffer, to safeguard.

_____

_____

_____

_____

_____

Recall Feeling PITIED

For something you lack, in looks, in stature, in worldly means. If they knew what you employ to maintain dignity, they'd be better prepared for reversals in their own life.

_____

_____

_____

_____

_____

Recall Feeling PUNISHED

Blamed, faulted, made to pay. On what grounds, theirs or
yours, fairly or unfairly? Knowing the difference is up to
you. Learn, and live whole.

_____

_____

_____

_____

_____

Note Often QUARRELSOME

Quick to disagree, pick a fight, argue over every last
detail. Moody in default mode, nothing pleases you or
them. Step one is to neutral ground.

_____

_____

_____

_____

_____

Note Being RASH

Hair-trigger reactions. Jumping to preset conclusions, in
the absence of forethought. Compare outcomes to your
less impetuous moments.

_____

_____

_____

_____

_____

Note Times of REGRET

"If only" you hadn't acted irresponsibly. "If only" you had chosen another path. But every life zigzags. This one is your muddle; learn from each turn.

_____

_____

_____

_____

_____

Recall Feeling REJECTED

Unchosen, spurned, didn't measure up. By whose criteria? Look around. Find a playing field where your assets are valued. You are worthy, just as you are.

_____

_____

_____

_____

_____

Recall Feeling RESENTFUL

It's a slow poison that sours and sickens you. While the target of your rancor is out living abundantly, not suffering. Save your own life. Let it all go.

_____

_____

_____

_____

_____

Recall Being RIDICULED

For height or weight or accent. For core heritage or faith or family. It stings because we crave acceptance. "They" only get to direct one life, theirs. And you direct yours.

_____

_____

_____

_____

_____

Recall Feeling RUDE

Tactless, impatient, lacking in common courtesy. To what end? Self-indulgence, mainly. Why alienate others? You depend on them for many of your own needs. Self-edit.

_____

_____

_____

_____

_____

Recall Feeling SCARED

Of standing up, of speaking out. Startled by the unexpected. Afraid of what lurks in shadows. Can't run, can't hide. Whittle it down to size. Address it piecemeal.

_____

_____

_____

_____

_____

Note Times of SELF-BLAME

Didn't know, messed up, forgot again. Can't ever get it right. Scolding yourself just adds one more brick to carry. Set it down, lighten the load.

_____

_____

_____

_____

_____

Recall Feeling SELF-CONSCIOUS

All eyes on you, too public. Feeling judged, found lacking. Narrow your scope. Find one friendly face, one positive attribute. Give yourself credit.

_____

_____

_____

_____

_____

Note Times of SELF-PITY

It's all stacking up against you; can't ever catch a break. Note that others bear silent scars, too, and struggle with the human condition. Ease up.

_____

_____

_____

_____

_____

Recall Feeling SKEPTICAL

What you hear sounds fishy, overinflated promises. Search for some kernel of truth. Make your best next moves from there.

_____

_____

_____

_____

_____

Recall Feeling SPLINTERED

Like shards of a mirror. Roles collide: child, parent, sibling, neighbor, friend; work-life, home-life, others. Wrap yourself in peace and wholeness. Move on, rewoven.

_____

_____

_____

_____

_____

Recall Feeling STRANGE

Can't quite name it. Push and pull of forces; ill at ease, unfocused. Scan each body part, each thought, each memory. Until it all sorts out.

_____

_____

_____

_____

_____

Note Times of SUFFERING

Personal pain or mistreatment, broader inequality or injustice. Hopes dashed, dreams fade. Somebody somewhere has right and just goals. Link up with them.

_____

_____

_____

_____

_____

Recall Feeling TENSE

Stiff neck, sore shoulders, erratic heart rate, shallow breathing. Your body believes what your mind replays. Change the script to a hopeful version.

_____

_____

_____

_____

_____

Recall Feeling TERRIFIED

The dark night, the brutal foe, the unrelenting torment. When will the morning come? Preserve a corner of your heart for hope. Dwell there.

_____

_____

_____

_____

_____

Recall Feeling UNAPPRECIATED

Your ideas are dismissed, your help is devalued. No one is grateful. Fill your own tank. Appreciate your own efforts, towards your own goals.

Recall Feeling UNCHOSEN

Disregarded, overlooked, set aside. Your wishful hopes are dashed. No one escapes this wrenching pain. You can move on in amicable company elsewhere.

Recall Feeling UNDESERVING

Of notice, of acclaim, of the plum position. Of the love you seek. Shift your focus to give notice and give love, if only to a pet. You deserve all you seek.

Recall Feeling UNGRATEFUL

Everyone else has plenty. You don't have enough, didn't get what you want. Can't fake it. Count instead: air, life, shelter, beauty, freedom. Gratitude comforts.

_____

_____

_____

_____

_____

Recall Feeling UNSAFE

Direct threats to you or actual assault. Ambiguous fears of being stalked or being scapegoated. Seek safety in numbers; or courage to disregard danger, and live wide open.

_____

_____

_____

_____

_____

Note Being UNYIELDING

Can't see it their way. Won't give in or give ground. But rigid is stuck, narrow. Shift to open mind and open heart. Reap the rewards.

_____

_____

_____

_____

_____

Note Times of VENOM

Like a volcano erupting, it incinerates. Lashing out against mistreatment, or hate. Make the verbal visual, to see its damage. Practice containment.

_____

_____

_____

_____

_____

Recall Feeling WARY

Things are not what they seem. Undercurrents can set you off balance. Back away or delay, if possible, until clarity prevails to light the way forward.

_____

_____

_____

_____

_____

Recall Feeling WORRIED

When will it all crash? How will you ever cope? Nothing you try seems to work. Lower the smokescreen, search. Trust in finding dozens of options.

_____

_____

_____

_____

_____

Recall Feeling WOUNDED

By words, by actions, by slights; cut to the quick. How could they? Then remember when you once did, sent slings and arrows. Being solely human.

_____

_____

_____

_____

_____

Note Times of YEARNING

For something you can't have. For more than you've got right now. If it's meant for you, see how each small step opens new doors right for you.

_____

_____

_____

_____

_____

Note Times of ZEALOTRY

Death grip on one's own beliefs. Boxed in, fanatical, railing against opponents. But truth can be a blend, a pyramid, to withstand assault. Listen, and revise.

_____

_____

_____

_____

_____

PART TWO:

Living the Wisdom

"It is only human nature to have a human nature." —Clifford Geertz, anthropologist

"I am not what happened to me. I am what I choose to become." —Carl Jung, psychiatrist

Introduction to Part Two

You are far more than what you own. You are far more than the job you do. Yet many of us devote most of our time to our purchases and to our work. Your work lets you provide for yourself and maybe your family. Your purchases help you design a life for yourself and your family. You and others benefit from your time and effort to make that happen. What matters most, though, is who you are. Now that you are more familiar with all that you are, glimmers of all that is possible begin to emerge.

Draw on your personal survey of the landscape of emotions from Part One to explore how to capture the wisdom that arises in your day-to-day life. See how you stand firm in situations that once rattled you. Notice how you let others be themselves without sacrificing yourself to them. You begin to recognize the gentle nudge of wisdom that accompanies you, to lead you towards the best life for you. It might appear as a synchronicity, hearing some news that you needed to complete a task. It might appear as a coincidence. You might, by some chance, meet the exact person who can open new doors for you.

Of course, you might instead face the reality of a closed door. No one likes to be blocked from their goals. Changing direction at that moment, though, can help you steer clear of unnecessary suffering. Say, for example, you had your heart set on fame and fortune. If you are meant to attain fame and fortune, be sure to live that life without unnecessary strife, without agonizing. If you are merely wishing for fame and fortune without any defined entry into that life, regroup and take stock of other ways to employ your skills and talents. Settle into being all that you are, without apology, in a world that needs you *just as you are*. Follow the cues that guide you towards knowing how and where to fulfill your dreams.

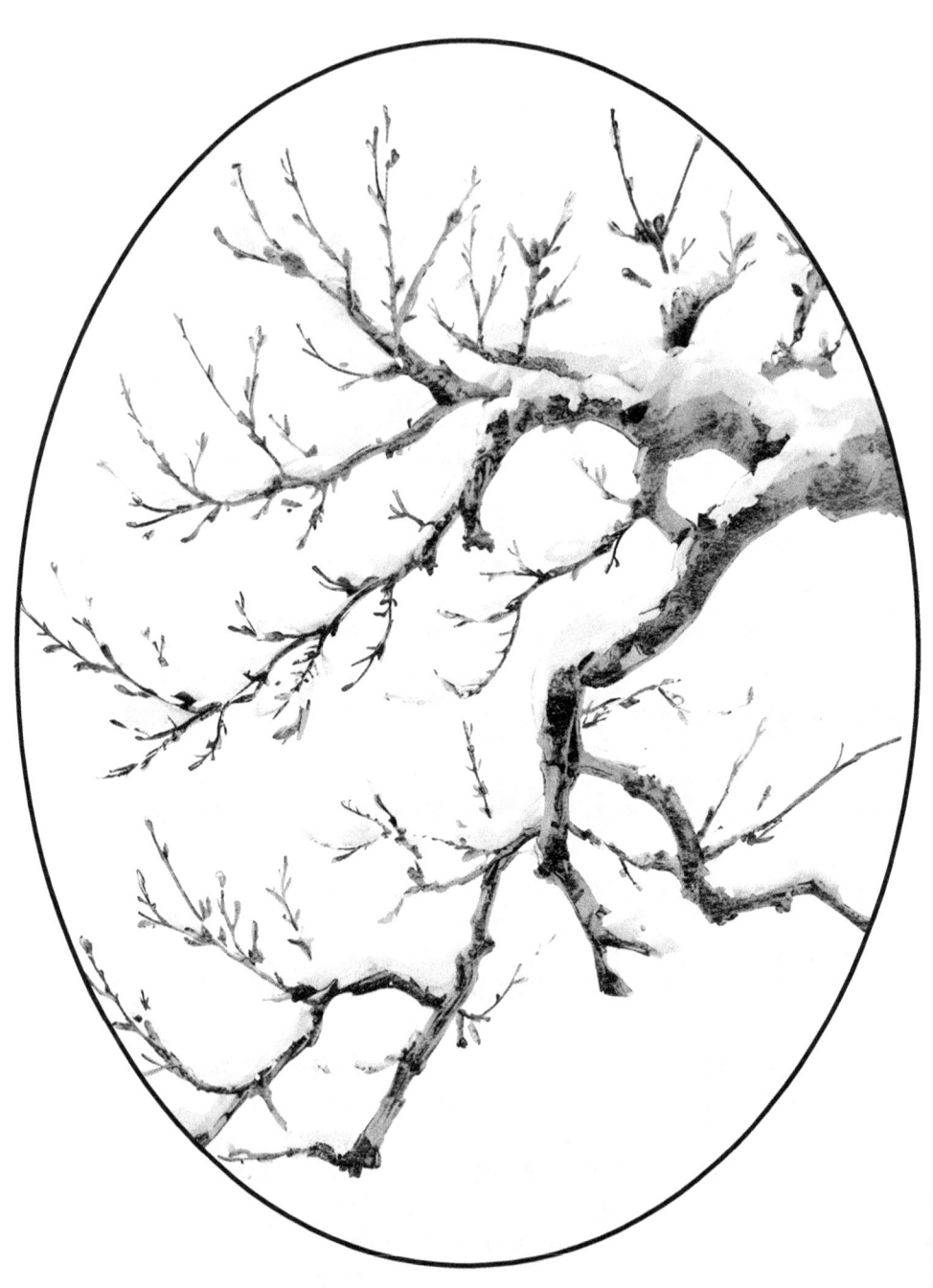

Chapter 3

✠ Resilience: Adjusting to Reality

"What we think is less than what we know;
What we know is less than what we love;
What we love is so much less than what there is."
—R. D. Laing, psychiatrist

Real world choices have real world consequences. Not all of them work to your advantage. You're not the only one to pay a price for stumbling along the way or being caught in a tangled web. Resilience is the capacity to stay afloat amid life's trials and torments. It is best practiced in small doses, then drawn upon when disaster strikes. You can rehearse in impersonal arenas before you turn your attention to the personal ones.

The more you own, the more often the need arises to service, repair, or replace each, at a cost. Yet you rarely anticipate these added costs when you fulfill your desires by adding to what you accumulate. The practice of surrender in small matters helps you build the capacity for surrender against great odds. You come to realize that you have responsibility even when you have no control. You are responsible for the things that break down, out of your control. The idea of control is often over-inflated.

In your personal life, you may feel added torment when reality throws you a curve ball. Unrequited love, family strife, did not win the prize, lost your job, accidents with injuries, an unplanned move to a less desirable location, and more. None are under your control. Railing against what already is, compounds your misery. What you rehearsed in small doses on impersonal matters you can employ when the stakes are higher.

Each reflection in the chapter gives you an opportunity to view life and all its puzzling moments from a fresh perspective, fine-tuned to reality. You are gifted with intuition and discernment for a reason. These help you expand beyond the logic of knowledge. Parts of your life are less well known and, like love, move in mysterious ways. Sometimes what appears to be a disadvantage brings you new lessons and opportunities. By staying curious, you stop overthinking every element of your day. You begin to notice the workings of a reality that few of us are taught to comprehend. You grow to be far more aware of the inexhaustible resources available for reconciling with the world, just as it is.

End the day with a purpose. *Slowly breathe in a sense of expansiveness, aware that you are far more than you believe moment to moment.* Read the selected reflection and listen as it echoes through you. Let the words settle you into sleep and help you awaken with renewed purpose. Recall the exact moment when others displayed that version of resilience, whether you met them in person, on social media, or in print. Aim to employ that same measure of resilience yourself.

Relive the times you naturally reached for a coping strategy rather than a stress response. Then extend that stretch into further resilience, beyond your usual tendency to do so. Move just as readily with courage and boldness when that response is needed to secure peace and justice. End the day by recording on page 77 something notable from your self-study, perhaps in a shift towards some helpful, creative resolution. Remember, you claim as your own every layer of resilience you uncover and develop.

1st

Self-soothing is a skill rarely taught. Yet needed daily. In distress, soothe yourself first, then problem-solve, for best possible outcomes.

2nd

You can't control the wind. Or other people's opinions, or accidents, or tragedies. Not your fault? Then no self-blame. It wasn't personal.

3rd

Counting what you don't have makes you suffer. If you count what you do have, you feel bountiful. The feeling of gratitude will lift your spirits.

4th

Is this a good thing? Maybe. Is this a bad thing? Maybe. Life is shifting sand, difficult to define. Don't rush to judgment, leave room for it to unfold.

5th

Thrive like a child thrives. Play in the sunshine, sing out loud, cry when you're hurt. Lean on others when you need help. And laugh!

6th

Appearances can be deceiving. Smiles can hide sorrow, anger can mask shame. Others misjudge you? You misjudge, too. Pause to see clearly.

7th

There are hundreds of afflictive emotions. We live them one by one, or layered. And tame them by art, music, dance, and study. Or nature and beauty. Choose what soothes you.

8th

No one is at their best all the time, being warm and loving and kind. When you miss the mark, don't add a layer of censure. Just get back on track.

9th

We are all vulnerable; there is no shame in it. That happens at the places where you were wounded. Heal yourself with love and tenderness.

10th

Calm is not passive; calm is aware. Of all the motives, the minefields, the opportunities. This helps us act with a measured response, not frantic.

11th

You don't need to learn what you already know. Lessons arise to bolster your weaker skills. Perhaps when people annoy you, you learn to soften.

12th

Each generation has crises that seem insurmountable. You balance the stress with resilience, optimism, and community. Even in small doses at the start.

13th

You can't stop the storm, but you can take shelter. That shelter is inside you, untouched. It is built sturdy and furnished with care, your own.

14th

No one comes into this world alone. We stay connected. You take care of some, some take care of you. Now, and always, balanced caring.

15th

When tragedies abound, look for a new anchor in time. Try saying: "It already is what it is. Now what?'" Regroup, revise, reconnect, and recreate.

16th

In times of crisis, your self-definition changes. Beyond the fear and anxiety, you see yourself as more. More capable, more open, and more giving.

17th

What we think matters; what we say matters. What we trust matters; what we do matters. Write your life story with care, embellished with passion.

18th

Things don't always work out. You can't be good enough or smart enough or rich enough to guarantee it. Buffer the crash, adjust expectations.

19th

Doing well when life is smooth? Try coping well when life is rough, that builds resilience. You discover untapped strengths yet unused.

20th

We are planners and schemers and dreamers. But life advances Life's agenda. Feeling undone? Given time, dream new dreams.

21st

Who are you when you close the door, close your eyes? Use this silent minute to meet yourself, and live your whole truth. At home, at peace.

22nd

Every phase of life has challenges. There is no map; you stumble through, intact. Until a new day dawns full of promise, resolve, and deeper values.

23rd

All around you looks bleak, besieged, broken. Tune into your own heart and find the spark. You are what the world needs now. Meet the moment.

24th

All best intentions, for what is right and good and just and true, get ambushed by fragile, fickle human nature. Start over, anew, renewed.

25th

The needs seem overwhelming today. Injustice abounds, also poverty, hunger, and illness. Help just one person, that is enough. For now.

26th

You shoulder the burdens all week long. Take time today for self-care. Move it to the top of your list. Breathe, soothe, unwind, and recover.

27th

Uncertainty can be a trigger or a lever. It can trigger fear and doubt, or leverage access to new visions. Learn, expand, and grow, undaunted.

28th

We can feel helpless when we see someone suffer, yet being a witness matters. You notice, show up, and speak out. That turns tides.

29th

Many before us rose up with valor, against great odds. Find a champion to emulate. Then draw from your own deepest well, inspired.

30th

At core, we are all one tribe. Insults are painful threats used to separate us. Give voice to your cherished values. Reach out, repair, and rebuild.

31st

No one can take from you what you give yourself. Give abundantly: love, respect, kindness, comfort, and forgiveness. Until it overflows!

PERSONAL NOTES

_____

_____

_____

_____

_____

_____

_____

_____

_____

_____

_____

_____

_____

_____

_____

_____

_____

_____

_____

_____

_____

_____

_____

_____

_____

_____

_____

_____

Chapter 4

✥ Depth: Life as the Master Teacher

"Just turn up, full of love, and do the work."
—Sister Dr. Jenna, author

"Whatever the question, Love is the answer."
—Wayne Dyer, author

"Love your neighbor, no exceptions."
—Quaker Tenet

"We are stardust, wrapped in love molecules."
—Mikki Franco, author

Chapter 4 gives a shorthand introduction to wisdom teachings. These deeply introspective reflections guide you in learning how to withstand life's challenges. There's more to you than you could ever fathom. Yet who among us can measure up to every test the world demands of us? Learning when good enough is good enough is a life-saving skill. You begin to realize that you are now taking stock with your own measuring tools.

Only the wisest sages remain contented, regardless of circumstances. You and I must practice. We practice until the intensity of our immediate reactions begins to lessen. We practice until the time it takes us to rebalance after being upset diminishes. The practice of each reflection helps build a reservoir that enriches you every time you draw from it. With the deepening of your own clarity comes a breadth of compassion for the entire human condition. Notice deeper, richer changes as you continue to practice. The changes in you ripple out to the world around you.

End the day with a purpose. *Slowly breathe in a sense of expansiveness, aware that you are far more than you believe moment to moment.* Read the selected reflection and listen as it echoes through you. Allow that there is more to your existence than meets the eye. Let the words settle you into sleep and help you awaken with renewed purpose. Be comforted by the natural synchronicities that link you to others. Appreciate how many commonalities there are among people all across the globe. Express gratitude for the warmth and kindness given to you from unexpected sources.

End the day by recording on page 87 something notable from your self-study, as you follow in the footsteps of the wise. Remember to claim as your own every layer of the depths of your own existence. These are often hard won. Every new layer opens you further to the wholeness of you. That is life's greatest gift to you and your greatest gift to your world. Stay curious!

1st

You are here for a reason.
Don't try to live someone else's reason.
Share your own gifts.
Hold a mirror for others, not a magnifying glass.

2nd

Each moment is either a blessing or a lesson.
Receive the blessing and give thanks.
Or learn from the lesson, without self-blame.
We are all learning, day by day.

3rd

You awaken with a routine day ahead.
Then find it in shambles around you.
Survey the damage. Assess the options.
You must live life on Life's terms.

4th

Emotions are messengers, inviting you to notice.
Don't get swamped by the surge of feelings.
Ride the waves of emotions. Stay on your board.
Then think it through and act rightly.

5th

Mistakes are simply multiple attempts at mastery.
No one is master of all there is to know.
We are here to share what we have with others.
As they are meant to share with us.

6th

Getting duped by the far-too-clever is easy.
Their tactics aren't even in your mindset.
True discernment is an active pause to reflect.
What lies below the surface is highly informative.

7th

You don't get credit for the sunrise or the sunset.
Many setbacks were out of your hands as well.
Others contributed to your successes.
Share credit, defuse blame.

8th

No one can decide for you.
Listen to opinions from both admirers and critics.
Ignore what has no meaning for you, at this time.
Trusted advisers help bolster your own true path.

9th

You are both ordinary and extraordinary.
No insult can harm you, being human, ordinary.
No praise can inflate you; you are already extraordinary.
Everyone is remarkable in their own way.

10th

Life deals each person a hand of cards.
No one gets the whole deck, 100% of everything.
Sometimes you want the hand your neighbor got.
Your only option is to play the hand you're holding.

11th

Constant worry takes energy, wears you down.
Worry is wasted, solves nothing. Thinking suffers.
For best health, practice the long pause.
Eyes closed, slow breaths for three minutes. Repeat often.

12th

Every family has a story to tell.
Some swash-buckling romps, some dramatic comedies.
Others are fraught with sorrow and tragedy.
You have one role to play. Play it with integrity.

13th

Whatever gives you pain causes you to suffer.
Pain arises from both external and internal sources.
If you berate yourself for each pain, you suffer twice.
You only control the self-inflicted kind. Resist doubling it.

14th

We see our visions come to life, in our mind's eye.
Until reality delivers us a dose of the unexpected.
Cursing and wailing do not change reality.
You can reorient and find a new way through.

15th

Always seeking more, better, faster, finer things?
For what purpose? Will it satisfy your longings?
Just this once, practice being content, having enough.
Aware that you have plenty, far more than most.

16th

We feel confident when life favors us.
Far too often, though, we face major setbacks.
Each disaster brings new opportunities for character study.
To learn to be heroic in your own life.

17th

Everyone remembers their first heartbreak.
A broken heart affects your health and emotions.
One heartbreak after another? Take time to heal.
Soften at the broken places, where others can relate.

18th

Life can be wonderful. Life can be tragic.
Both are true, in different times, or circumstances.
Don't make it personal.
Face it, drawing on wisdom and fortitude.

19th

Anger is a signal that an obstacle is in your way.
A rapid adrenaline surge rises to help you move it.
But acting angry is voluntary and purposeful.
Collect yourself. Evaluate the need before responding.

20th

Nothing stays static. Life is constant change.
The good in a good day will not endure.
The bad in a bad day will not last.
Breathe through the ups and downs of both.

21st

How easy it is to go along with the crowd.
Even when the crowd lives by different values.
Being excluded was a mortal risk at the dawn of time.
Stand apart just this once. See, you will survive.

22nd

Maintaining self-confidence is like walking across a seesaw.
All seems steady until you are careening out of control.
Take the leeway of stepping into unknown territory.
You will either expand your skill set or find an advisor.

23rd

You want to be exactly who you are.
Let others be exactly who they are.
Without apology, blame, or expectation.
There is no equivalence. Each person is unique.

24th
Sorrow is an uninvited companion on your journey.
Sometimes you feel irresponsible or unloved.
Sometimes you lose out, lose faith or lose hope.
This tender place connects you to everyone.

25th
Healthy practices require a sense of balance.
We want to trust without being played for a fool.
To share our vulnerabilities without being scorned.
Start with just enough, not too much; add from there.

26th
Staying calm and content is like working a muscle.
The more you exercise it, the stronger it gets.
You don't even need an hour. Begin with three minutes.
Every time you feel off-balance, pull back and readjust.

27th
Not every encounter in life suits you.
Consent to bear the burden of discomfort when needed.
Consent to make a difference when possible.
For yourself, or for another.

28th
Getting what you want when you want it is a luxury.
All around the world, few people enjoy such privilege.
Life teaches us to tolerate doing without.
At least for the time it takes to replace, or find a substitute.

29th

It is gut-wrenching when we lose our way.
But wandering is part of the journey.
Simply add wonder as you wander.
About the beauty of the earth, and all the people in it.

30th

Every emotion can be energizing, or debilitating.
Take discontent. Left to fester, it can sour you.
Or it can spur you on to positive change.
The power to live a self-satisfying life is yours.

31st

At the end of the day, grasp what truly matters.
Did you love and serve, as best you were able?
Within the limits of your time, your talents?
That is the measure of a life well-lived.

What's Next?

*"Nothing has changed, but everything has
shifted—in a good way."*
—Susan Mallery, novelist

This practice of self-study is now in your own hands.
You can continue to examine emotions and mood states beyond those given here. As you read, talk with, or listen to others, take note of the feelings they mention or those they elicit in you. Expand your journal entries with these newest additions. There is much to be gained from this exercise that will enrich your life. There is nothing that you are not. Stay open to all that you are. Move on to new heights and depths!

PERSONAL NOTES

_____

_____

_____

_____

_____

_____

_____

_____

_____

_____

_____

_____

_____

_____

_____

_____

_____

_____

_____

_____

_____

_____

_____

_____

_____

_____

_____

_____

Perfectly Imperfect

"Everyone is a flawed person. That's what being a person is. Todo. El. Mundo.

With an emerald, the more inclusions, the more cracks and defects, the more beautiful it can be. An authentic emerald is beautiful for its flaws. They call it perfect imperfection."

You are not here to be perfect. None of us are. You are here to live. And help live."

—Matt Haig, novelist

Suggested Readings

Benson, Herbert (1997). *Timeless Healing: The Power and Biology of Belief.* New York: Scribner.

Borysenko, Joan (1988). *Minding the Body, Mending the Mind.* New York: Bantam.

Bourgeault, Cynthia (2018). *Love is the Answer, What is the Question?: Selected Writings and Talks* 2016 ~ 2018. CreateSpace Publishing.

Doty, James (2016). *Into the Magic Shop: A Neurosurgeon's Quest to Discover the Mysteries of the Brain and the Secrets of the Heart.* New York: Avery.

Ekman, Paul (2016). *Nonverbal Messages: Cracking the Code, My Life's Pursuit.* Paul Ekman Group.

Fox, Nathan A. (Ed.) (1994). "The Development of Emotion Regulation." *Monographs of the Society for Research in Child Development,* Serial No. 240, Vol 59. Chicago: University of Chicago Press.

Gibson, Lindsay C. (2020). *Who You Were Meant to Be: A Guide to Rediscovering Your Life's Purpose.* Far Hills, NJ: New Horizon Press.

Goleman, Daniel (1995). *Emotional Intelligence: Why It Can Matter More Than IQ.* New York: Bantam Books.

Gross, James J., & Ford, Brett Q. (Eds, 2024). *Handbook of Emotion Regulation,* 3rd Ed. New York: Guilford Press.

Hanson, Rick (2009). *Buddha's Brain: The Practical Neuroscience of Happiness, Love & Wisdom.* Oakland, CA: New Harbinger Publications.

Kabat-Zinn, Jon (2007). *Arriving at Your Own Door: 108 Lessons in Mindfulness.* New York: Hachette Books.

Kabat-Zinn, Jon (2013). *Full Catastrophe Living (Revised Edition): Using the Wisdom of Your Body and Mind to Face Stress, Pain, and Illness.* New York: Bantam Books.

Luthar, Suniya S. & Cicchetti, Dante. (2000). "The construct of resilience: Implications for interventions and social policies." In *Developmental Psychopathology*, 12(4): 857–885.

Moore, Thomas (2000). *The Original Self* (audiobook). New York: Harper Collins.

Palmer, Parker (2004). *A Hidden Wholeness: The Journey Toward an Undivided Life.* San Francisco: Josey Bass.

Pert, Candace B. (1997). *Molecules of Emotion: Why You Feel the Way You Feel.* New York: Scribner.

Siegel, Dan (2022). *IntraConnected: The Integration of Self, Identity, and Belonging.* New York: W. W. Norton & Co.

Tippett, Krista (2016). *Becoming Wise: An Inquiry into the Mystery and Art of Living.* New York: Penguin Books.

Williamson, Marianne (2016). *Tears to Triumph: The Spiritual Journey from Suffering to Enlightenment.* New York: HarperOne.

Acknowledgements

My first thanks are sent to W. Andrew Collins, my dissertation chair at the University of Minnesota, who insisted that the written word isn't truly communication until it is clear.

Ongoing thanks to my team of advisors, with me every step of the way in this endeavor: Ronald Jacobson, Robert Maldonado, Janis Sanchez, Lisa Tedeschi, Suzan Thompson, Eleanora Woloy, and Weare Zwemer.

Deepest thanks to my trusted reviewers: Bruce Bischoff, Daniel Fleagle, Joanne Haag, Laurel Llobell, Aimee McCullough, A. Kimberly Owens, Maria Urbano, and Catherine Walsh, co-reader extraordinaire.

With special thanks to illustrator Jeff McLure for his extraordinary talent, good humor, and boundless patience, to photographer Bruce Bischoff for his stunning photos and for answering all my five-alarm concerns about digital media with measured aplomb, and to C. Steve Vinson for his belief in this project from the very start.

There would be no book without the commitment of Maureen Carroll at Anamcara Press. Immeasurable gratitude to you for your unstinting encouragement of new writers into the literary community! From our first contact, you warmly supported me on this journey and removed every obstacle that might interfere. I am forever in your debt!

And to Vicki Julian, esteemed editor, my most sincere thanks! There is a level of trust that must exist between author and editor to succeed. At every step, your clear-sighted guidance bolstered me and helped turn this manuscript into the book it is today. Now on to the next endeavor!

Sustaining Beliefs

We are born into corporeal bodies in a material world, seeking meaning and purpose on our journey. We welcome guidance and direction most especially during times of adversity, confusion, reversals, and travail. We value insights from friends and family as well as advisors on this search. Yet we must honor our unique personal path as the ultimate gauge of our own well-being.

To become fully adept at facing life's obstacles, we might strive to be brave, bold, smart, strong, relaxed, confident, independent, fierce, and real. All worthy individual qualities, but there is meant to be more. In addressing and nurturing our "interior self," we begin to align with larger universal values that have withstood the test of time: such as Love, Joy, Peace, Patience, Kindness, Goodness, Gentleness, Generosity, Compassion, Understanding, Acceptance, Tolerance, Gratitude, and Mercy.

Life, meanwhile, delivers chaos, crises, roadblocks, setbacks, disasters, disturbances, failures, and loss. The challenge at hand is in how to incorporate these into our life, our psyche, using our deeper values to maintain a steadfast equanimity. We carve out time to practice, seeking inner wisdom, a beacon towards a safe harbor. We take time to be fully alive, in every way, in every moment of every day, with everyone we encounter. And after we stumble, we begin again.

—*printed originally in* The Write Bridge Journal, *Summer 2024 edition, Grief and Comfort.*

About the Author

Suzanne (née Kasper, Getz) Gregg, PhD, holds a doctorate in Developmental Psychology from the University of Minnesota. Her career spans academic, public sector, and private sector settings. She held faculty appointments at Penn State University (Tenured) and Eastern Virginia Medical School (Retired). She served as education specialist and clinical supervisor with Comprehensive Mental Health Services for the City of Virginia Beach. She recently retired as a clinician in solo private practice for 28 years.

Photo by Erin Mullinax

Raised in a military family, she spent her formative years in Japan. Returning stateside, she found her niche among poets and writers. She believes she has learned as much about the human condition from remarkable authors as she has from renowned teachers and researchers.

While raising her own family, she counseled other parents in raising theirs and trained students to continue the work. Active in the pursuit and dissemination of knowledge, she spoke to schools and communities and presented at conferences both nationally and internationally. On this path, she has gained as much as she has given. She currently serves as Senior Consultant at Gregg Consulting Services. Her goal in retirement is to enjoy more of this wondrous world, by staying curious.